THE NO-NONS

Read *How to Choose a Discount Stockbroker*

- If you want to get started in the stock market
- If you're already an investor and want to save money
- If you want to know how much you can save
- If you want advice on how to do it yourself

NO-NONSENSE FINANCIAL GUIDES:

How to Finance Your Child's College Education
How to Use Credit and Credit Cards
Understanding Treasury Bills and Other U.S. Government Securities
Understanding Tax-Exempt Bonds
Understanding Money Market Funds
Understanding Mutual Funds
Understanding IRAs
Understanding Common Stocks
Understanding the Stock Market
Understanding Stock Options and Futures Markets
How to Choose a Discount Stockbroker
How to Make Personal Financial Planning Work for You
How to Plan and Invest for Your Retirement
The New Tax Law and What It Means to You

NO-NONSENSE REAL ESTATE GUIDES:

Understanding Condominiums and Co-ops
Understanding Buying and Selling a House
Understanding Mortgages
Refinancing Your Mortgage

NO-NONSENSE LEGAL GUIDES:

Understanding Estate Planning and Wills
How to Choose a Lawyer

NO-NONSENSE FINANCIAL GUIDE

HOW TO CHOOSE A DISCOUNT STOCKBROKER

Phyllis C. Kaufman
& Arnold Corrigan

LONGMEADOW PRESS

How to Choose a Discount Stockbroker

Cover art © 1985 by Longmeadow Press.
Design by Adrian Taylor. Production services by William S. Konecky Associates, New York.

Published December 1985 for Longmeadow Press, 201 High Ridge Road, Stamford, Connecticut 06904. No part of this book may be reproduced or used in any form or by any means, electronic or mechanical, including photocopying, recording, or by any information storage and retrieval system, without permission in writing from the publisher.

ISBN: 0-681-40243-1

Printed in the United States of America

0 9 8 7 6 5 4 3 2

In memory of
H. Mendel Kaufman, Esquire
and
Bessie Kaufman Shir, with love

TABLE OF CONTENTS

PART 1
THE DISCOUNT
STOCKBROKER

1

WHAT IS A DISCOUNT STOCKBROKER?

A *stockbroker*, or broker, is someone who is licensed to buy and sell securities on the stock exchanges and to charge a commission for performing the service.

A *discount stockbroker* is one who will buy and sell the securities at commission rates that are lower than those charged by non-discount (full-service) firms.

A discount stockbroker offers little or no investment advice, little or no research and only minimal frills. Their main function is to buy and sell securities for knowledgeable investors at a reduced rate.

What Can I Buy from a Discounter?

What kinds of securities can I buy through a discount stockbroker? Just about anything that's traded on the stock exchanges, and a bit more. Here's a general list:

- Stocks
- Corporate bonds
- Municipal bonds
- Zero-coupon bonds
- U.S. government securities
- Stock options
- Stock index options
- Commercial paper
- Banker's acceptances
- Tax-exempt bond funds

and some offer trading in

- Mutual funds

How Many Discount Stockbrokers Are There?

There are currently over 100 discount stockbrokers in the United States, including several with branches nationwide, and the field is rapidly expanding. However, as we shall see, not all discount brokers are alike, and the services they offer vary greatly. So, while the field may be small, the need to shop is still great.

2

HOW MUCH WILL YOU SAVE?

Will you really save substantial amounts by using a discount stockbroker? Will the savings be worth it?

Of course, the first answer depends on what you mean by substantial. But without quibbling over words, the answer is—yes, you can save very meaningfully by using a discounter, whether you measure the savings in dollars or in percentages.

As for whether it is worth it, in later chapters we'll compare the discount brokers with full-service brokers and make some suggestions as to your own possible strategy in using either or both.

Commission rates on stocks often depend on the price per share as well as on the total amount involved, so any generalizations have to be approximate. One point is clear: among the discounters, rate schedules vary considerably, and you should shop carefully based both on rates and on available services. Also, while we will talk about the "typical" commission rates charged by full-service brokers, those firms also do not have uniform rates, though they tend to cluster rather closely.

For example, let's say that you purchased 100 shares of XYZ Corp. at a price of 50, for a total cost of $5,000. As rates stood in early 1987, the trade would probably cost you a commission of about $85 at a full-service broker. At the leading discounters, the commission might range from about $35 to $49.

If you had bought 1,000 shares of FXF Corp. at 25, for a total cost of $25,000, your commission at a full-service firm would have been about $400. At the discounters, it probably would have been between $85 and $135.

5

Here are more examples of typical 1987 commissions and the percentage savings you might have realized—but remember that all figures are approximate:

Size of Trade	Approx. Commission at Full-Service Broker	Range of Commissions at Leading Discount Brokers	Percentage Saving
100 shs. @ 20 (total $2,000)	$ 50	$ 30–49	40%–2%
100 shs. @ 50 (total $5,000)	85	37–65	56%–24%
500 shs. @ 20 (total $10,000)	195	50–92	74%–53%
1,000 shs. @ 25 (total $25,000)	400	85–134	79%–66%
1,000 shs. @ 50 (total $50,000)	550	105–185	81%–66%
2,000 shs. @ 50 (total $100,000)	875	175–285	80%–67%

Note that on smaller orders in the area of $1,000 or less, the discounters may *not* save you money. Several of them have minimum transaction fees, which may be $35 or thereabouts. This is not unreasonable, since it probably costs the firm something like that amount to process even the smallest trade, considering the paperwork and computer time involved. But if you have an active account at a full-service broker, there's often no minimum commission, and the commission on a small "odd-lot" transaction can be well below $35, depending on the firm's policy.

To shop intelligently, first make an estimate of what the average size of your transactions in stocks is likely to be. Then work out the commission schedules, preferably using a small calculator (as was done in drawing up the above table), or simply ask the firms what the commissions would be on a few typical trades in your range. Some firms give you full commission schedules that do most of this work for you; others give you formulas where you have to do the math yourself.

We've talked only about stocks, but you can also save with the discounters on other types of securities. On listed *options*, which are a popular way of speculating with a limited investment, you will probably save from 30% to 50%, on the average, by using a discounter instead of a full-service broker.

On *bonds*, the savings will depend very much on the size of your order and which broker you use. For corporate bonds listed on the exchanges, some full-service brokers charge a flat commission of $5 per $1,000 bond. Some discounters charge the same $5 figure, while others reduce it, especially on larger orders. On U.S. Treasury securities, a separate and lower schedule often applies at both the full-service brokers and the discounters, with the lowest rates of all applying on short-term Treasury bills and notes. If you expect to be dealing in these frequently, ask about the rates.

3

A BIT OF HISTORY

A discount broker, as you can see, charges you lower fees for executing your trades. Why is discounting such a talked-about phenomenon? To understand how discounters evolved, you need to understand a bit of history.

In the Beginning

The stock exchanges have been heavily regulated by the government since the 1930s. The U.S. Securities and Exchange Commission (SEC) administers the federal securities laws and supervises all stock exchanges. The exchanges are also self-regulated, with strict trading rules and strict rules of conduct to be observed by members.

It's expensive to become a *member* of an exchange. A membership or *seat* on the New York Stock Exchange can cost as much as $300,000 or $400,000. And before anyone is permitted to purchase a seat, he or she must pass strict scrutiny as to character, experience and knowledge of the securities business.

Remember that the exchanges themselves do not buy or sell securities. They are merely marketplaces where people go to transact business in securities. They operate on their reputations for honesty and integrity, and they guard their reputations carefully.

May Day

Prior to 1975, all stockbroker commissions on sales or purchases were fixed according to uniform schedules set by the exchanges. Every member firm charged exactly the same fee for executing a particular trade. Brokers engaged in fierce competition for clients, but the competition centered on their services and the quality of advice they offered.

And the commission schedules were very profitable for the brokers, especially on large trades. Although it doesn't cost a broker much more to process a large trade than a small one, the quantity discount built into the commission schedules was quite limited. The large orders placed by institutions were a bonanza for many brokers.

However, as time passed, these large institutional investors (pension funds, insurance companies, banks, mutual funds, etc.) began to rebel against the commissions they were paying to the brokerage firms. The institutions began to trade off the exchanges, through brokers who weren't exchange members and who were able to charge less because they weren't bound by exchange rules. The New York Stock Exchange found its monopoly position shrinking and its best customers drifting away.

Then on May 1, 1975, "May Day" to the securities industry, the New York Stock Exchange, under pressure from the SEC and this new outside competition, ended the era of fixed commissions forever and a new era of "negotiated commissions" began.

The results were not what the average investor might have wished. The institutions, who had bargaining power, did immediately negotiate much lower commissions for themselves, but the commissions paid by most individuals remained the same, or even rose, depending on the circumstances.

The Rise of the Discounters

It was not until a new group of *discount brokers* developed that the average trader realized the savings the SEC sought on May Day. The discount brokers began to offer brokerage service—that is, the pure execution of buying and selling orders—for reduced rates, without the expensive research and advice offered by the full-service firms.

Enter the Banks

The field of discount brokerage was further expanded in 1983, when banks were permitted to form discount brokerage divisions or establish arrangements with outside discount brokers for their customers.

4

HOW DO FULL-SERVICE STOCKBROKERS WORK?

Regulation

All stockbrokers, whether full-service or discount, are strictly regulated by the SEC. Every broker knows that if a customer is treated unfairly, the customer can complain to the SEC—or to the National Association of Securities Dealers (NASD) or the various stock exchanges, all of which are considered self-regulatory organizations.

Full-service Brokers

Full-service brokers, such as Merrill Lynch, Prudential-Bache, Shearson Lehman Brothers, Paine Webber and others, are household names because of their extensive advertising campaigns. In addition to these and other giant national firms, there are some excellent smaller regional and local firms.

Registered Representative

As a customer of a full-service firm, you deal with an individual account executive or *registered representative* (so-called because he or she is *registered* with the stock exchanges and the NASD, an association that establishes rules and standards governing the behavior of its members). The *registered rep* or *RR* —whom we will refer to simply as *your broker*—draws on the volume of research and recommendations from the firm's research department to make suggestions regarding your portfolio of investments.

Sometimes this works well for the client; sometimes it doesn't. The firm's research and recommendations may be good or not so good. The individual broker may be more or less experienced, and may or may not have a talent for telling the good from the bad, and for adapting the firm's ideas to the needs of individual clients.

There's usually no simple way to tell how well a brokerage firm, or an individual broker, has done for clients in the past unless you know someone who has had excellent experience with a particular broker. By all means talk to that broker and see if he or she might be right for you. If you walk into a brokerage firm off the street and have a broker assigned to you, be careful. If you have doubts about the broker, or if your first experiences aren't satisfactory, don't hesitate to talk to the firm manager or branch manager about making a switch. See if the conversation gives you a clue as to whether you need merely a different individual broker, or perhaps a completely different firm.

We recommend dealing only with an individual broker with at least five years' experience, so that he or she will have lived through both good and bad markets and learned how to react to both.

The Broker's Conflict

You must also remember that most individual brokers in full-service firms are in a position that involves a potential conflict of interest. For better or worse, the average broker is paid as a salesperson—whose compensation depends primarily on the amount of brokerage commissions generated from buy or sell orders. The more orders a broker executes, the more money he or she makes.

The broker may also be under pressure to recommend certain investment products or packages where both the broker and the firm make higher-than-average commissions. These very often concern speculative or new issues, where the risk is greater than normal, but the commission is high. Under these pressures, it's not always easy for a broker to give impartial advice.

12

Discretion

Some full-service brokers offer an arrangement under which they have total control over your account. This is known as giving *discretion* to the firm to buy and sell for you (at their *discretion*). In a discretionary account you need to exercise extra care, since professionals can make mistakes in any case, and in the case of a broker there is the extra temptation, conscious or not, to lean toward an approach that generates higher commissions.

Ask Before You Leap

Whatever kind of arrangement you are entering into with any kind of broker, discount or full-service, don't begin until you've asked every question you can think of about the firm's experience and procedures. And in the case of a full-service broker, make sure to check the individual broker's experience, and the ability of the broker and the firm to meet your needs, preferences, and objectives. Don't hesitate to ask hard questions about commission rates; and if you don't get clear answers, go elsewhere.

5

ADVANTAGES AND DISADVANTAGES OF DISCOUNT STOCKBROKERS

Research

Full-service stockbrokers offer plentiful research services and advice for their clients. You get help in making your investment decisions (though the advice isn't necessarily good). Discount stockbrokers offer no research assistance. You have to get your help or advice elsewhere.

Churning

Full-service stockbrokers pay their employee brokers a percentage of each commission on trades they execute. This carries a potential conflict of interest because the individual broker's pay depends on how many purchases and sales he or she makes for clients. The more trades, the more money the broker will make. (See Chapter 4.)

At the extreme, this can lead to charges of *churning*, a term used to describe a situation where the broker is trading on a client's behalf merely to increase the amount of commissions earned.

Discounters avoid this conflict completely by paying their employee account representatives a straight salary. No percentages are paid on trades executed.

Salespersons

All individual stockbrokers, whether with a full-service or discount firm, must be registered with the National Association of Securities Dealers (NASD) and with the stock exchanges. All must pass examinations to make sure that they know the trading rules and other matters. However, there the similarity largely ends. The individual brokers employed by full-service firms are salespersons, giving the client advice on the desirability of a security.

Discounters don't sell. All they do is execute trades—no research, no advice, no information. They carry out your bidding. The discount firms can offer lower commission rates because they save on research costs and because they don't pay a percentage of commissions to employee brokers.

Success and Selection

Your success at a full-service firm depends largely on which individual broker you select or which one is selected for you. If you're like most of us and don't have a reliable recommendation for a broker, then you take pot luck and you will be matched with whoever is available when you walk in the door. Very often this is the least experienced broker, fresh from training, who hasn't been through the up and down swings of the market that give a broker seasoned judgment.

Obviously, this problem doesn't exist with a discount firm. Most of their business is simply order-taking by telephone. If you do walk in, the person who helps you is merely executing your orders, so his or her prior experience really doesn't matter.

6

HOW TO CHOOSE THE RIGHT DISCOUNT STOCKBROKER

Not all discount stockbrokers offer the same services. But since none of them offer advice, individual personalities aren't important. And, since most discount business is by telephone, convenience to your home or office is irrelevant.

Courtesy and Convenience

What is important is reliable service. And since much of it will be given by telephone, it's important for a discount broker to provide courteous and prompt telephone service, usually via a toll-free "800" number.

Some discounters offer telephone service 24 hours a day, 7 days a week, while others limit accessibility to regular business hours. If you need the ability to place orders at odd hours, pick a broker who gives you that service.

Commissions

Discounters do *not* all charge the same commissions for identical transactions. Quite the opposite—the commission schedules vary widely. It's essential that you compute the actual cost of a few of your typical trades to see which firms offer you the best deal. Would your typical trade be 100 shares of a stock at 20 (total $2,000)? Or 10 shares at 50 (total $500)? Or larger quantities? Or are you interested in options, or futures, or bonds? Check the commission schedules. Be careful to check the *minimums* to see if you will actually realize a saving if many of your trades are small.

16

Quotations

Most discount brokers will provide customers with the latest available trading prices (quotations) of securities by telephone. Some offer this service 24 hours a day, 7 days a week.

Choice of Account Representative

Some discount brokers allow you to request a specific account representative each time you call with a question or trade. Others don't offer this service and connect you with the first available representative.

If individual personalities are important to you, you might tend toward a firm that offers you this service. However, since the discounters don't offer advice, we don't consider this too important a feature.

Making a Trade

What is important is how your orders are handled, both in terms of courtesy, efficiency and timing.

Of course, your call should be answered promptly and you should be immediately connected to a representative. Any questions you have regarding the prices of various securities should be promptly answered.

Placing an order should be no more complicated than giving the representative your name and account number and trading instructions. You can usually place any type of order you wish, but you must be careful to be specific in your instructions. Make sure that your order is read back to you and verified, in order to avoid mistakes.

Confirmation

Discount stockbrokers are usually highly computerized, and they can often confirm your trade during your telephone conversation. If not, it's advisable to be at a place where they can call you back to confirm. Confirmation should take a very brief period of time, usually no longer than 5 minutes.

A written confirmation ("confirm") of your trade should promptly follow after execution. In addition, all of your account activity should be reflected in your monthly statement. Make sure to check both documents for accuracy. If you are not getting clear, prompt confirms and statements, consider switching to another firm. You'll need clear records for your own investment purposes and at tax time.

Recording

Many discount firms make a tape recording of all telephone orders. You should be aware of the fact that you are being recorded and understand that this is for everyone's protection, in case of error.

Timing of Dividends and Interest

Most discounters give you one check each month to cover any interest or dividends earned on securities in your account. Some offer this service each week. It's obviously to your advantage to get your money sooner rather than later, but one distribution a month isn't unreasonable.

Securities Investor Protection Corporation

The accounts of all customers of discount stockbrokers are protected through the Securities Investor Protection Corporation (SIPC), a nonprofit corporation established in 1970 under the Federal Securities Investor Protection Act.

SIPC is not a governmental agency and it receives all its funding from member broker-dealers. Like the FDIC or FSLIC in the banking industry, its purpose is to protect investors in the securities markets from the possible financial failure of a member. While SIPC does not provide protection against falling stock prices or investment mistakes, it does insure the customer's securities held by the firm up to $500,000 in case the firm runs into financial difficulties. (Cash in the account is insured only up to $100,000.)

7

TYPES OF DISCOUNT BROKERAGE ACCOUNTS

There are a few different basic types of brokerage accounts. However, not every discount broker offers each of the accounts we will discuss, and the services offered on each type of account may vary from broker to broker. So it's important to decide which services are most important to you before deciding which firm is best for you.

Cash Accounts

A cash account is the simplest type of brokerage account. Many discount stockbrokers allow you to open a cash account with no deposit, either of cash or securities. A cash account allows you to buy securities for cash, which simply means that you pay in full for what you buy—in contrast to a margin account, where you can borrow part of the cost of the securities.

A few firms, however, do not permit cash accounts and allow you only to open a margin account, with a required deposit that may be as much as $5,000 (in cash or securities). This is a convenient way of excluding smaller customers, and the margin accounts are probably simpler and more profitable from the standpoint of the firm.

Margin Accounts

If you want to be able to borrow against your securities, you can open a *margin* account, which carries several advantages and some dangers. Under stock exchange rules, you must deposit at least $2,000 in cash or securities to open a margin account, and some firms set a higher minimum. You can then borrow up to 50% of the value of common stocks in the account, and higher percentages on bonds, all the way up to 90% in the case of U.S. government securities.

When you *buy on margin* you are borrowing right at the beginning to finance your purchase of a security. For example, if you buy 200 shares of a stock selling at 50 (total cost of 200 times $50 equals $10,000), you would only be required to put up $5,000 of the cost, and could borrow the other $5,000 from the brokerage firm. You can look at this as a way of economizing on your cash, or you can look at it as a way of buying more of a given security than you would otherwise be able to.

The Dangers of Margin

But beware. Because you have bought twice as many shares with a given amount of cash, you have increased your risk. You can now make twice as much profit or lose twice as much. In the first place, you will be charged interest on the amount you borrow. Second, what if the price of your stock drops from 50 to 40? You now have securities worth only $8,000 in the account, and you still owe the firm $5,000, plus any interest charges that may have accumulated. Your *equity* in the stock—your real ownership share—is only $3,000 (that is, $8,000 minus $5,000). In percentage terms, your equity is now only 37.5% of the market value of the stock.

Generally, depending on the rules of the individual brokerage firm, when your equity gets down to 40% or 35% of the market value of your securities, the firm will ask you to put up additional cash or securities. This is called a *margin call*. Alternatively, you may *sell* securities to raise your equity to the maintenance level that the firm requires. Under New York Stock Exchange rules, in no case can your equity be allowed to drop below 25%; but, as noted, most firms ask you to take corrective steps before you get too close to that point.

Borrowing on Your Securities

The credit arrangement built into a margin account can also be used for straight borrowing. Let's say that you have paid in full for the stock in the above example, and that it is sitting in your margin account with a market value of $10,000. You have the right to borrow up to $5,000 in cash, on demand, with the stock serving as collateral. In effect, you have a completely flexible $5,000 credit line, and you are charged interest only on the exact amount you choose to borrow, for whatever period your "debit" continues. It's one of the cheapest and most effective forms of credit available to an individual.

A margin account can be a convenience at times even if you plan to pay in full for your purchases and don't expect to do any serious borrowing. If you have just made a purchase, and find it inconvenient to get a check to the broker within the required period (see "Settlement Date" below), the borrowing power you have on the securities already in the account may be enough to cover the purchase until you can conveniently get your check in—especially since, with your margin account, you are only required to put up 50% of the purchase cost.

Margin Interest Rates

If you expect either to buy on margin or to borrow against your securities, the interest rate you are charged is most important, and it varies considerably from broker to broker.

To get money to lend to you, the broker takes your securities to the bank as collateral and borrows at the *brokers' call loan rate*, which is one of the lowest interest rates in the market, and usually below the *prime rate* that banks charge to high-quality business borrowers. On your margin account, certain brokers will charge you as little as ½ of 1% above the call loan rate, which is a remarkable bargain. Others charge substantially more of a premium, or link their charge to the *prime* rate, which is likely to work less well for you. So if you expect to use margin credit, shop carefully before you open a discount brokerage account, and use a broker who charges low interest rates. It will be worth it to you later on.

Many people don't realize just how advantageous margin borrowing can be. Why do we term it a re-markable bargain? Here's an example. In mid-1985, the margin rate at certain brokerage houses dipped *below 10%*. By comparison, the rate on mortgage loans was roughly 12%, automobile loans were generally 13% or more, and it might have cost you anywhere from 18% to 21% for a cash advance on your Visa or MasterCard. So, as we said, borrowing against your securities is a bargain, and it's probably more flexible than any other loan arrangement. (However, under the Tax Reform Act of 1986, the interest you pay in 1987 and later years may not be fully tax-deductible—see your accountant or tax advisor.)

Profiting from Your Cash Balance

Check with the brokerage firm to see what happens when cash comes *into* your account, either from a sale of securities or from dividends or interest earned on your securities.

Of course, you can always instruct that the cash be paid out to you. In the case of dividends and interest, most firms have a system by which any amounts that come in can be paid out to you automatically either weekly or monthly.

But if the cash remains in the account, and if the amount is large enough to matter, you want to be sure that the cash is earning interest. Most discounters pay interest in some form on credit balances, but some only pay when the balance exceeds a specific amount, such as $1,000. Find out the balance required and how the interest rate is calculated.

Some brokers link the rate they pay to the current rate on Treasury bills and try to stay competitive with money market accounts. Some *sweep* all sizeable cash balances into a money market fund either daily or weekly.

Checks, Credit Cards, Bells and Whistles

Some brokerage firms offer *asset management accounts* that seem to provide the ultimate in convenience and versatility. Usually there's a minimum size for such an account, perhaps $5,000, and it's intended for someone who owns securities and leaves them on deposit. Typically, dividends and interest, and the proceeds of any sales, are swept into a money market account where they earn a good interest rate.

The account carries regular margin privileges. Moreover, there may be an arrangement where, with a credit card and/or checks, you can draw not only on any cash in the account, but also on your margin borrowing power. If you like the idea of packing a lot of credit power in your wallet or pocketbook, this is a way to do it.

Option Accounts

If you expect to buy or sell options, the brokerage firm is required to verify that these usually speculative items are suitable for you. An option account is similar to a margin account, and often these two are combined into a single margin account.

Settlement Date

In this chapter we've discussed many of the features of cash and margin accounts. Now we'll turn to some other points you need to know.

Settlement date on any ordinary stock transaction is five business days after *trade date* (exactly one week later, unless a holiday intervenes). Settlement date is the date when the *firm* "settles" the trade with the opposing broker. On that day the firm pays for any stock you have bought, and receives the security on your behalf; or it delivers a stock you have sold, and receives payment.

So whatever money you must pay on a purchase (100% of the cost if cash, 50% if on margin) is due at the brokerage firm by the settlement date. Conversely, if you've sold a stock, the firm normally won't make payment to you before settlement date.

You should note that some discounters require that there be sufficient funds in your account on the day your buy order is executed, not at settlement five days later. This ties up your cash for a longer period, which may matter to you. If so, shop around for a more favorable arrangement.

Street Name

Most discounters prefer that securities left with the firm be registered in *street name*, that is, in the name of the brokerage firm, rather than in your own name. This ties in with the requirement by some firms that all accounts be margin accounts, in which securities are normally held in street name.

While some people are hesitant about this arrangement, we think it's safe enough in view of the fact that all accounts are insured by SIPC (see Chapter 6). Street name is really a much more convenient arrangement, unless you intend to hold a stock for a long time and want all dividends and other mailings to come to you directly.

Remember that if you want to sell securities registered in your own name, and you are holding stock certificates, you will have to deliver the signed stock certificates to the broker. Even if the firm is holding the certificates for you in safe deposit, you will still have to provide them with a signed *stock power*.

To encourage you to use street name, many discount firms charge you a fee for having securities registered and delivered in your name. And the delivery may take several weeks. All in all, we feel comfortable recommending that you keep your securities in street name, assuming that your account is of a size where you are fully insured by SIPC (that is, up to $500,000). The street name arrangement makes for convenience, speed, and also safety. Remember, the broker is insured for lost or stolen securities. Are you?

How Accounts Are Registered

Brokerage accounts can be opened in individual names or in various other ways, which we will list briefly.

Individual Account

An individual can open an account in his or her name solely.

Joint Tenancy with Right of Survivorship

In this account, both parties actually own the entire contents of the account, and the one who survives on the death of the first ends up as the sole and complete owner outright. This type of account is most often used by married couples or by relatives as an alternative to giving a gift.

Because both parties own the entire account from the beginning, the contents of the account pass to the survivor directly.

Tenants in Common

This account resembles a joint tenancy, but with no right of survivorship. This means that each tenant in common can bequeath his or her share as he or she desires.

Corporation or Partnership

Corporate or partnership accounts are usually permitted by discount brokers. However, note that in accounts other than individual accounts, additional documentation is usually required.

Trust

It is common for an investment account to be opened in the name of a trust. The broker is likely to request a copy of the trust agreement.

Uniform Gifts to Minors Act

Most discount brokers allow custodial accounts for gifts given under the Uniform Gifts to Minors Act to be established. Note that the Social Security number to be given on such an account is that of the minor, and not of the adult custodian.

Individual Retirement Accounts

Most discount brokers offer what are called *self-directed IRAs*, since you have complete freedom to direct the investments. Competition in this part of the business has helped the customers; at one time, the brokerage firms charged substantial fees for setting up and maintaining this type of account, but now many of the firms offer IRAs with no setup or maintenance fees at all. You pay the usual commissions on purchases or sales of securities in your IRA, and your cash balances earn interest between investments.

Margin trading is not permitted in an IRA account, and most firms also bar option trading in such accounts.

Keogh Plan Accounts

The same rules that apply to self-directed IRAs also apply, in most discount brokerage firms, to *Keogh plans* (self-employed retirement plans). However, there's an extra problem that you should be aware of. While IRAs are quite standardized, and don't vary much from broker to broker, Keogh plans come in considerable variety. They all have to be approved by the IRS, but they can vary in flexibility and in the options they offer, particularly for a self-employed individual with employees who must be covered. Before signing up for any Keogh plan, you should review it carefully with your tax advisor.

Switching Brokers

It is usually reasonably easy to transfer your account between one full-service or discount brokerage firm and another. However, the process can be time consuming, often taking several weeks. There's usually no good reason for this, other than the fact that moving your account out is a very low priority item for the broker you are leaving. Try to leave on good terms, and urge someone at a managerial level to help you move your account out promptly. If you don't get a reasonable response, announce your intention to complain to the New York Stock Exchange or the SEC (Securities and Exchange Commission). Since your account may have to remain inactive during the transfer period, there's no reason to put up with undue delay. Normally, an unpaid debit balance in a margin account can be shifted from one firm to another, assuming that the receiving firm has agreed and that the account is otherwise in good shape.

8

PLACING AN ORDER

When you place an order with a discount or full-service broker to buy or sell a stock, you have certain choices. You can buy or sell *at the market*, which means at the best price the broker can get for you at that time. Or you can place a *limit order*, under which you buy only if the price dips to a specified level, or sell only if it rises to a specified level.

If you place a limit order, it can be for that day only, for a week or a month; or it can be *open* or *good till canceled (GTC)*, which means that the order stays on the books until it is executed or until you cancel it.

Less commonly used, but worth knowing about, are *stop orders*, which can be used to protect a profit or limit a loss. A stop order becomes a market order when the price of a stock reaches or sells through a specified point amount. For example, let's say that you have bought a stock at 40 and the market price rises to 55. You might then place a *sell stop* order at 50 to protect yourself against the possibility of a sharp market decline and assure yourself a minimum profit of around 10 points. If the market price dips to 50 or below, your sell stop order will become a market order to sell, and would be executed immediately at the best price available—presumably close to 50, though in a rapidly falling market it might be substantially lower. Similarly, if you bought the stock at 40 and it did not do well, you might place a sell stop order at 35 to limit your loss to around 5 points.

There are also *stop limit* orders. With these, your order becomes a *limit* order rather than a market order once the market price goes through the stop price. This is intended to give you some control in a situation where the market price is moving so rapidly that an ordinary stop order might be executed far away from the stop price (since it has then become a simple market order and may be competing with many other market orders).

Not Held Orders

What if you want essentially to place a market order, but the stock is thinly traded, and you are afraid that the broker on the floor of the exchange will have to bid the price of the stock up substantially to fill your buy order, or sell the price down to fill your sell order? In this case it may be useful to place a *market not held order*. The phrase means that the broker is not *held* to take the first available offer or bid, but has discretion to wait and possibly to negotiate if the broker thinks that he or she can thereby get a better price. If the broker decides to wait and his or her judgment turns out wrong, you have to live with the error. If you expect to place many large orders, particularly in less active stocks, you should find out when and on what basis a broker is willing to accept not held orders. Some firms would rather avoid these, since the floor broker may spend extra time waiting and watching.

Odd Lots

Stocks normally trade in units of 100 shares. These are called *round lots*. There are also arrangements that let you buy *odd lots* of from 1 to 99 shares. In some cases you may pay ⅛–point less on a sale.

9

HOW TO USE A DISCOUNT STOCKBROKER—STRATEGIES

If you're an experienced investor, comfortable in making investment decisions, then you're ideal for a discount broker. You must remember, however, that if you've been satisfied with the guidance and recommendations of your stockbroker, and if he or she has given you excellent advice in the past, you should take time and consider whether the potential discount savings will be worth the loss of your broker's recommendations. Good advice can be worth a lot of money, and excellent suggestions can easily make up for the difference in commission rates.

Some experienced investors try to retain the best of both worlds by having accounts with both a full-service broker and a discount broker. They feel that if they're giving the full-service broker enough business to pay reasonably for his or her services, there's no reason why additional trades shouldn't be done through a discount firm. This is all the more workable if the investor's total activity is sizeable and many of the trades are large.

If you're a novice investor, too, you may want to stop and consider before you plunge completely into the world of discount brokerage.

Strategy for the New Investor

We suggest the following strategy for the new investor. Select a good and reliable full-service stockbroker. Ask your friends and relatives for a recommendation and try to choose one who is seasoned—that is, someone who has been through at least one major up market and one major down market (use at least 5 years of brokerage experience as a guideline).

Of course, if you aren't a large customer, and if your portfolio and ability to invest are modest, you will not get the full attention of the full-service broker as you would if you had a $500,000 account.

But that really doesn't matter, because the reason we recommend starting with a full-service broker is as a learning experience. Ask questions of your broker. Try to learn what he or she considers important. Understand the security analysis process. Try to get on as many of the firm's mailing lists as possible. This will give you an idea of how investment recommendations are made.

Later on, when you're with a discount broker, you will have to substitute other reading material that you pay for, but you will have a better idea of what you are looking for and how to analyze the facts you read. (See Chapter 11.)

During this learning process, you should try to read as much as you can so that you can talk to your broker intelligently. It might even be a good idea to take a course at a local college on investing and/or finance.

Then, after you understand how your broker operates, begin to make selections for yourself. Ask your broker's advice and find out his or her recommendations and comments on your choices. Once you have begun to understand the process and what to look for, start to invest little by little with a discount broker. Try your hand at it and compare your results with those you are achieving with the help of the full-service broker.

You may want to stay with this dual approach for a long time, or you may feel that you are ready to do it all yourself. The timing of the switch will be up to you.

10

THE MUTUAL FUND
ALTERNATIVE

For many of us, making investment decisions is not an easy process.

Buying mutual funds is an excellent way to invest without the pressures of individual securities decisions. Several discount brokerage firms now offer you simplified ways of buying and selling mutual fund shares. Before we get into the details of how this works, let's take a brief look at mutual funds.

What Is a Mutual Fund?

A mutual fund is a pool of money from many investors, which is professionally managed for maximum efficiency and economy as a single large unit. The best-known type of mutual fund is probably the money market fund, where the pool is invested for complete safety in the shortest-term income-producing investments. Another large group of mutual funds invest in common stocks, and still others invest in long-term bonds, tax-exempt securities, and more specialized types of investments.

The mutual fund principle has been so successful that the funds now manage over $400 billion of investors' money—not including over $250 billion in the money market funds. (For a full discussion of mutual funds, read the No-Nonsense Financial Guide, *Understanding Mutual Funds.*)

Advantages of Mutual Funds

Mutual funds have several advantages. The first is *professional management*. Decisions as to which securities to buy, when to buy and when to sell are made for you by professionals. The size of the pool makes it possible to pay for the highest quality management, and many of the individuals and organizations that manage mutual funds have acquired reputations for being among the finest managers in the profession.

Another of the advantages of a mutual fund is *diversification*. Because of the size of the fund, the managers can easily *diversify* its investments, which means that they can reduce risk by spreading the total dollars in the pool over many different securities. (In a common stock mutual fund, this means holding different stocks representing many varied companies and industries.)

The size of the pool gives you other advantages. Because the fund buys and sells securities in large amounts, commission costs on portfolio transactions are relatively low. And in some cases the fund can invest in types of securities that are not practical for the small investor.

The funds also give you *convenience*. First, it's easy to put money in and take it out. The funds technically are *open-end* investment companies, so called because they stand ready to sell additional new shares to investors at any time or buy back (*redeem*) shares sold previously. You can invest in some mutual funds with as little as $250, and your investment participates fully in any growth in value of the fund and in any dividends paid out. You can arrange to have dividends reinvested automatically.

Load vs. No-load

There are load mutual funds and no-load funds. A *load fund* is usually bought through a full-service broker or salesperson who helps you with your selection and charges a commission (load)—typically (but not always) 8.5% of the total amount you invest. This means that only 91.5% of the money you invest is actually applied to buy shares in the pool.

In a *no-load fund,* you have to make your own choices without the help of a broker or salesperson, but 100% of your investment dollars go into the pool for your account. It is primarily this type of fund that is handled by certain of the discount brokers. They charge a small service fee for handling your mutual fund purchase, but on a purchase of any size, this fee amounts to less than 1% of the value of the shares, and more than 99% of your dollars actually go to work for you.

The Daily Mutual Fund Prices

One advantage of a mutual fund is the ease with which you can follow a fund's performance and the daily value of your investment. Every day, mutual fund prices are listed in a special table in the financial section of many newspapers, including the *Wall Street Journal*. Stock funds and bond funds are listed together in a single alphabetical table, except that funds which are part of a major fund group are usually listed under the group heading (Dreyfus, Fidelity, Oppenheimer, Vanguard, etc.).

Using a Discount Stockbroker to Buy Mutual Funds

While it's basically a great advantage to be able to buy and sell shares of no-load funds without paying any commission, the process has its drawbacks. Some funds will take your purchase order by telephone, but others won't, which means that you mail a check which may take days to arrive at the office of the fund or its service bank. If the market goes up during those few days, you pay a higher price for the fund shares than if you had been able to buy immediately.

When you want to sell or redeem your shares, the problem is repeated and accentuated. Almost all the funds require that any redemption order be in writing, which means a delay of a few days after you make your decision (unless you are near enough to visit the fund office in person, or unless you cut the delay to one day by using Express Mail). Moreover, on a redemption request it's usually required that your signature be *guar-*

anteed by a commercial bank or brokerage firm, which adds another obstacle to quick action.

Charles Schwab & Co., the largest discount brokerage firm, has come up with a mutual fund program that meets some of these problems, and several other discount brokers are following with similar offerings. Schwab has worked out arrangements with about 200 no-load funds permitting Schwab to place orders for its customers by telephone. The customer can place an order to buy or sell any of these funds on any business day simply by calling Schwab before 4:00 P.M. New York time.

For a mutual fund purchase, Schwab requires that the money be in the customer's account before the order is placed. On the other hand, the mutual fund shares can be bought on margin (by putting up as little as 50% of the cost), which is an option that isn't open to the mutual fund investor who buys directly from the fund.

As of early 1987, here's how the Schwab fees for this service worked out for different size purchases:

Amount of Purchase	Service Fee	
	$	As % of Price
$ 1,000	$ 20.00	2.0%
5,000	44.00	0.9
10,000	58.00	0.6
50,000	138.00	0.3

Obviously, you can still save money by doing it yourself. But if the no-load funds you want to buy are handled by Schwab or another discount broker (and some no-load funds are still *not* available through the brokers), then you may find the extra fee justified by the convenience and by the ability to buy and sell your fund shares promptly.

Some no-load fund investors find it hard to accept the idea of paying any fee on purchase of their shares. Obviously, if you are buying fund shares to put away and hold for the long term, and if you aren't concerned with day-to-day market movements, you may be perfectly happy dealing directly with the fund.

PART II
HOW TO CHOOSE
INVESTMENTS

11

READ, READ, READ, AND RESEARCH

Investing has elements of both art and science. The art takes practice, but you can make progress on the science if you are willing to take the time to read and study.

What must you know in order to become an investor in securities? In one sense, very little. You can, if you wish, go to any full-service stockbroker, explain your financial situation and objectives, and rely on his or her advice. Or, if you have a large amount to invest, you can ask for investment advice and management from an investment advisory firm or bank trust department.

But even if you intend to rely strongly on outside advice, the more you understand about investments, the better off you will be. You want to be able to explain your objectives intelligently to a professional, and you need to understand what the professional is recommending. As time goes by, you need to be able to judge whether your investments are going as planned, and whether the professional is doing the job he or she is supposed to do.

Be a Wise Investor

Actually, the decision to go it alone with a discounter is not as momentous as it may seem at first. No matter with whom you trade, any investor must be well informed and aware in order to judge objectives and results. A wise investor must be up to date on the latest developments in the economy and the world. You must actively participate.

Investment research involves looking at the whole world, often from a fresh and different viewpoint. Your thinking must be

- *alert* to news and new developments
- *flexible* enough to adjust rapidly when conditions change
- and *thoughtful* enough to consider all information seriously without jumping to conclusions.

Read

If you want to read further on investment subjects, the supply of available information is overwhelming. With critical decisions to be made every day regarding the movement of billions of dollars, investment managers and full-service stockbrokers spend vast amounts for the best data available, and a whole industry has developed to supply information, statistics and opinions on every conceivable type of investment.

If you are using a discount stockbroker, you may have to do some legwork. The discount brokers, as we've pointed out, generally don't supply research information or advice. However, we suspect that competition may bring some changes in this area. While we don't expect the discount brokers to set up their own research operations, some are beginning to work out ways of channeling outside research information to their clients.

For the present, you may have to look elsewhere for your education. Numerous books are available in your local bookstore or library. Go to the investment section, and do some browsing.

And don't neglect the information to be found on the newsstands. *Forbes* magazine (twice monthly) makes good reading, and *Barron's* weekly is another good source of articles. *Money* magazine (monthly) carries many articles on investments, and you will also find interesting articles in business magazines that are less oriented toward investments, such as *Business Week* and *Fortune*.

Information on Specific Companies

When it comes to information on individual companies, you may have to look in different directions. Much information is available from the companies themselves. Your local library may carry the statistical and research material compiled by the industry's two leading statistical and news sources, Moody's and Standard & Poor's.

Moody's and Standard & Poor's both publish encyclopedia-like manuals that include histories and descriptions of thousands of companies, and reams of statistics. There are daily or weekly updates to keep the information completely current.

If you want a quick picture of a company, both services publish individual pages on all major companies providing condensed descriptions and statistics. These not only offer a surprising amount of data, but also give you a clue as to what the experts regard as the most important facts—the two pages (front and back) function like a short course in the essentials of security analysis. If you don't have access to these individual company descriptions through your broker or library, you might try to get access to a local business school library.

Mutual Fund Information

There are several publications that compile figures on mutual fund performance for periods as long as 10 or even 20 years, with emphasis on common stock funds. One that is found in many libraries in the *Wiesenberger Investment Companies* annual handbook. The Wiesenberger yearbook is the bible of the fund industry, with extensive descriptions of funds, all sorts of other data, and plentiful performance statistics. You may also have access to the *Lipper—Mutual Fund Performance Analysis*, an exhaustive service subscribed to mainly by professionals. It is issued weekly, with special quarterly issues showing longer-term performance.

On the newsstands, *Money* magazine has a regular mutual fund section, with plentiful performance figures; *Barron's* weekly has quarterly mutual fund issues in February, May, August and November; and *Forbes* magazine runs an excellent annual mutual fund survey issue in August or September. (For additional sources, see the No-Nonsense Financial Guide, *Understanding Mutual Funds*.)

These sources (especially Wiesenberger) will also give you descriptions of the funds, their investment policies and objectives.

Hot Tips

There's one source of investment advice we haven't mentioned. What about all those "hot tip" investment suggestions that almost all of us have gotten at times from friends and relatives? Well—your friends and relatives aren't necessarily wrong. It's always possible that you know someone who is knowledgeable about a particular industry or a particular company.

But remember that the investment field is filled with professionals who work full-time screening information and following up possible investment opportunities. It's hard for an amateur to compete in this field without great care and hard work. Ideas that promise easy rewards probably also carry hidden risks. In investing, there's little room for miracles.

12

WORDS AND PHRASES

In this chapter we've included a few points of interest that didn't seem to fit anywhere else. Here they are, in no particular order.

Bulls and Bears

No discussion of the stock market could be complete without some reference to bulls and bears. A *bull* is an investor who expects the market (or a particular stock) to go up; a *bear* is one who expects it to go down. The origins of the phrases aren't completely clear, but they probably derive from the way each animal fights. A bull lowers its head and tosses its enemy up in the air, while a bear rakes downward on its foe with its claws. A *bull market* is one that is going up, and a *bear market* is one that is going down.

Selling Short

If you are a "bear," and you think that the market (or a particular stock) is going down, how can you speculate on it? Nowadays that can be done through transactions in options or financial futures. But before these markets existed, the classic bear investment technique was *selling short*. Selling short or short selling means that you borrow a security and sell it to someone, in the hope that the price of the security will go down so that you can then buy the security back more cheaply and deliver it to repay the loan, making a profit. The technique is recommended to experienced investors only. In the securities industry, you are *long* a security when you own it, and *short* when you don't own it but owe it to someone.

Stock Splits

Stock splits are traditionally viewed as good news for stockholders. But they don't basically mean very much, and now people pay less attention to them than they used to.

Assume that a company has 5 million shares of stock outstanding, selling at around $80 per share, and management thinks that the stock might have better trading markets at the more modest price of $40 per share. The company splits the stock 2-for-1. Now there are 10 million shares outstanding. Each old share has been transformed into two new shares, and the stock is trading around 40. Earnings per share have automatically been cut in half, and the price-earnings ratio remains the same.

No one is really any better or worse off. But the split is usually taken as a signal from management that the company is doing well, and the price of the stock may rise a few points above 40 out of market enthusiasm. In addition, the stock split may be accompanied by a dividend increase—instead of cutting the dividend rate exactly in half, the board of directors may set it at a rate which gives stockholders an effective increase.

The reduced interest in stock splits in recent years is probably related to the greater dominance of institutional stockholders in the markets. The institutions know that a split doesn't really change their interest in the company, and they also know that they may pay relatively lower commission rates when buying or selling stocks that are higher-priced.

13

GROWTH, INFLATION AND COMMON STOCKS

To manage your own investments well, you have to be very clear about what your investment *objectives* are—what you are trying to accomplish. Let's start by discussing some basic principles and guidelines.

Risk and Reward

Investing generally involves a trade-off between risk and reward. The higher the reward you aim for, the greater the risks are likely to be. Most of us recognize this. Everyone knows that fortunes have been made by people who owned the stock of I.B.M. over the years. But fortunes have been *lost* in many cases by those who owned the stocks of other computer companies that didn't do as well. As we said, it's a trade-off.

Playing It Safe

You may not want to take the risk of a substantial loss, but it is just as much a mistake to think that you can avoid all risks by playing it safe. Sometimes there are hidden risks in the choices most people think of as safest and most conservative.

Money left in a low-interest bank savings account may seem perfectly secure. But inflation may eat away the real value (purchasing power) of that money every year. On the other hand, investing in the common stocks of leading U.S. corporations certainly involves some risk, but the results for millions of investors have proved well worthwhile. What is important in investing is to *know what the risks are*, to keep them as limited as you can, and be sure that the risks are reasonable in relation to what you are trying to accomplish.

The Problem of Inflation

The savings bank example serves as a reminder of the extent to which the value of money has shrunk over the last twenty years in the U.S. because of inflation. Obviously, inflation is one of the important factors to take into account in your investment planning.

The inflation rate has gone through wide swings in recent years. It reached double-digit territory (above 10%) in 1979 and 1980, then dropped sharply to below 4% in the 1983–1986 period. Inflation is hard to predict, especially since it depends in large part on political decisions. However, we think that the prudent approach is to assume that inflation is still a major problem.

The underlying causes of inflation in the U.S. are still largely with us. Federal budget deficits have been running at record levels. Consumers are encouraged to borrow and spend now and to repay later. It's hard to imagine inflation staying down at the 2% to 3% level that prevailed in the 1950s and 1960s.

Common Stocks and Inflation

Investors put money in the common stock of a corporation primarily because they expect the corporation to do well over time. If the corporation is profitable and grows successfully, the value of its shares also should grow.

But common stocks have an additional attraction—over the long term, they generally adjust to inflation. The companies behind the common stocks own factories, land, forests, oil reserves, railroads and a host of other properties. They may own valuable patents or technical skills. As inflation causes all prices to rise, the prices of these corporate assets rise also. And the persons who own the corporations—that is, the shareholders—benefit from this increase in value.

The market prices of common stocks often seem out of step with inflation, speeding ahead in some years and falling behind in others. But over the long run, common stocks have given their owners a double reward: they have adjusted to inflation, and they have provided an extra margin as the result of business growth and expansion.

Over the whole postwar period since 1947, money invested in common stocks (with dividends reinvested) has grown, on the average, by about 11% annually. Over that whole period, the rate of inflation (measured by the Consumer Price Index) has averaged around 4% annually. So common stocks have kept the investor, on the average, about *6% or 7% ahead of inflation.*

That 6% margin may not seem like a lot, but it really is. The following table shows how $1,000 will grow if invested at 6% over a number of years:

	Growth at 6%
Start	$ 1,000
After 1 Year	1,060
5 Years	1,338
10 Years	1,791
20 Years	3,207
30 Years	5,743
40 Years	10,286

And remember that the growth you see in the preceding table is growth *above* the rate of inflation—that is, growth in the *real purchasing power* of your money. So $1,000 invested actually triples in real purchasing power over 20 years. It's an impressive statistic.

Of course, just because this type of growth has been achieved in the past doesn't mean that it will happen in the future. But with good planning and understanding, this kind of result may be well within your reach.

However, you must remember that these figures represent long-term averages and that common stock prices can and will vary and fluctuate, sometimes sharply. Over the short run, many of these movements seem unpredictable. If you invest in the stock market, be prepared for the long haul. (For more information, see the No-Nonsense Financial Guide, *Understanding Common Stocks*.)

14

COMMON STOCK BASICS

When common stock investments are well chosen, they let you share in the growth and prosperity of leading American corporations and of the whole economy. Also, because you are a part owner of the corporation's properties and other assets, stocks can protect you against inflation over the long run as the corporation's properties grow in value.

But being an owner involves risks, and no one should invest in common stocks without understanding that there are risks. First of all, the corporation you invest in may not do well—which may mean that your research wasn't adequate, or it may be because even the best companies can sometimes run into problems that no one could have anticipated.

Second, the whole economy can go through periods of recession or rapid change which affect even the best companies.

Third, even if the company and the economy are both in fine shape, the price of your stock is subject to the broad waves of enthusiasm and disappointment that characterize the stock market, and to minor market fluctuations as well.

Since your object is to make your money grow over the long run, it isn't enough to know that you are buying the stocks of quality corporations. You also need to be sure that you are buying the stocks at attractive *prices*—prices that are reasonable relative to the values of the companies and to past experience.

There is always an element of judgment involved in trying to estimate the real underlying value of a company, seen either independently or in relation to other companies in the same industry or field. But such judgments can be made. As an investor in common stocks, your objective is to buy stocks for less than these real underlying values—or for substantially less than you estimate the company and the stock will be worth in the future, a few years down the road.

The Company Report

What if someone has recommended a particular stock to you? Or if you yourself have noticed some aspect of a company that makes you think it might be a good investment? One of the best sources of information is the company itself, and particularly its annual report.

If you don't have easy access to such reports through a library or brokerage office, find the company address in one of the manuals of companies published by Moody's or Standard & Poor's. (Your local library should have some type of reference manual available.) Write to the office of the secretary of the company and ask for the latest annual and quarterly reports to shareholders. Almost all companies will oblige.

The *annual reports* of most companies are useful documents, full of information. The primary purpose of the report is to tell you about the events and financial results of the latest year, and a careful reading will tell you a good deal about a company's business. If the company is in more than one basic business, it will give you some idea of the relative importance of the different segments, and of the results that each segment has been achieving. The text will discuss the company's earnings, and any special factors that have been affecting earnings. It should also give some indication of how management views the outlook for the coming year.

The *financial statements* give the figures behind the report, and professional analysts are likely to look at these statements before they consider anything else. It takes experience to understand the investment significance of the statements, but it's well worth an effort on your part to begin to gain an understanding of what they are all about.

We suggest that you start by writing to the New York Stock Exchange Publications Department, 11 Wall Street, New York, NY 10005, and ask to order their excellent booklet, "Understanding Financial Statements." (While you're writing, ask for a price list of their other publications for individual investors.)

Preferred Stocks

A *preferred stock* is a stock which has many of the qualities of a bond (see Chapter 15). A preferred stockholder is entitled to dividends at a specified rate, and these dividends must be paid before any dividends can be paid on the company's common stock; in most cases the preferred dividend is *cumulative*, which means that if it isn't paid in a given year, it is owed by the company to the preferred stockholder. If the corporation is sold or liquidates, the preferred stockholders have a claim on a certain portion of the assets ahead of the common stockholders.

But in exchange for an assured dividend, the preferred stockholder generally does *not* share in the progress of the company; the preferred stock is only entitled to the fixed dividend and no more (except in a small minority of cases where the preferred is *participating* and receives higher dividends on some basis as the company's earnings grow).

Many preferred stocks are listed for trading on the NYSE and other exchanges, but they are usually not priced very attractively for individual buyers. The reason is that for corporations desiring to invest for fixed income, preferred stocks carry a tax advantage over bonds. As a result, such corporations generally bid the prices of preferred stocks up above the price that would have to be paid for a bond providing the same income. For the individual buyer, the bond is often the better buy.

15

BOND BASICS

Unlike a stock, a bond is evidence not of ownership, but of a *loan* to a company (or to a government, or to some other organization). It is a debt obligation. When you buy a corporate bond, you have bought a portion of a large loan, and your rights are those of a *lender*.

You are entitled to interest payments at a specified rate, and to repayment of the full *face amount* of the bond on a specified date. The fixed interest payments are usually made semiannually. The quality of a corporate bond depends on the financial strength of the issuing corporation; rating agencies such as Moody's and Standard & Poor's publish detailed credit ratings of companies and individual issues.

Bonds are usually issued in units of $1,000 or $5,000, but bond prices are quoted on the basis of 100 as *par* value. A bond price of 96 means that a bond of $1,000 face value is actually selling at $960. And so on.

Many corporate bonds are traded on the NYSE, and newspapers carry a separate daily table showing bond trading. The major trading in corporate bonds, however, takes place in large blocks of $100,000 or more traded off the exchange by brokers and dealers acting for their own account or for institutions.

U.S. Government Bonds

U.S. Treasury bonds (long-term), notes (intermediate-term) and bills (short-term), as well as obligations of the various U.S. government agencies, are traded away from the exchanges in a vast professional market where the basic unit of trading is often $1 million face value in amount. However, trades are also done in smaller amounts, and you can buy Treasuries in lots of $5,000 or $10,000 through your broker (or without a commission directly from the Treasury or through one of the Federal Reserve Banks). U.S. government securities provide you with assured income and the ultimate in safety. (For more information, see the No-Nonsense Financial Guide, *Understanding Treasury Bills and Other U.S. Government Securities.*)

Municipal Bonds

Bonds issued by state and local governments are generally referred to as *municipals* or *tax-exempts,* since the income from these bonds has traditionally been *exempt from federal income tax.* Tax-exempt bonds are attractive to individuals in higher tax brackets and to certain institutions. The tax exemption on certain state and local bonds has been curtailed by the Tax Reform Act of 1986, but there is still a broad supply of such bonds that enjoy full federal tax exemption.

There are many different issues and the newspapers generally list only a small number of actively traded municipals. The trading takes place in a vast, specialized over-the-counter market.

As an offset to the tax advantage, interest rates on these bonds are generally lower than on U.S. government or corporate bonds. Quality is usually high, but there are variations according to the financial soundness of the various states and communities; here, as with private corporations, quality ratings are published by Moody's and Standard & Poor's. (For more information, see the No-Nonsense Financial Guide, *Understanding Tax-Exempt Bonds.*)

Convertible Securities

A *convertible bond* (or *convertible debenture*) is a corporate bond that can be converted into the company's common stock under certain terms. *Convertible preferred* stock carries a similar conversion privilege. These securities are intended to combine the reduced risk of a bond or preferred stock with the advantage of conversion to common stock if the company is successful. The market price almost always includes a certain premium for the conversion privilege. Many convertible issues are listed on the New York Stock Exchange and other exchanges, and many others are traded over-the-counter.

16

OTHER INVESTMENT CHOICES

Options

An *option* is a piece of paper that gives you the right to buy or sell a given security at a specified price for a specified period of time. A *call* is an option to buy, a *put* is an option to sell.

In simplest form, these have become an extremely popular way to speculate in the hope that the price of a stock will go up or down. If you are wrong, the option generally becomes worthless, but at least you know that the most you can lose is the price you paid for the option. In addition, many trading techniques used by expert investors are built around options; some of these are used to reduce risks rather than for speculation.

The markets for options are extremely active. The leading markets are the Chicago Board Options Exchange (CBOE), the American Stock Exchange, the Philadelphia Stock Exchange, and the Pacific Stock Exchange. There are now options related to the various stock market averages, making it easy to speculate on the direction of the whole market rather than on individual stocks.

Financial Futures—the Commodity that Is Not a Commodity

The commodity markets, where foodstuffs and industrial commodities are traded in vast quantities, are outside the scope of this book. But because the commodity markets deal in *futures*—that is, contracts for delivery of a certain good at a specified future date—

they have also, by a sort of historical accident, become centers of trading for *financial futures*, which, by any reasonable definition, are not commodities at all.

Financial futures were launched some years ago, beginning with futures in foreign currencies and interest rate futures. *Interest rate futures* are based primarily on the prices of U.S. Treasury bonds, notes and bills, and they permit an investor to speculate on the future direction of interest rates. It's also possible, using certain techniques, to use these futures as a way of offsetting or reducing some of the risks in a person's *other* investments, particularly bond investments.

More recently, a new entry has blossomed and become extremely popular: futures based on various stock market indexes. Like the options mentioned above, these allow an investor to speculate on the direction of the whole market rather than on individual stocks. And just as interest rate futures can be used to offset the risks in a bond portfolio, these futures can be used to offset and reduce the general market risk involved in owning a portfolio of common stocks. (For more information, see the No-Nonsense Financial Guide, *Understanding Stock Options and Futures Markets*.)

Rights

When a corporation wants to sell new securities to raise additional capital, it often gives its stockholders *rights* to buy the new securities (which may simply be additional shares of stock) at an attractive price. The *right* is in the nature of an option to buy, with a very short life. The holder can use (*exercise*) the right or can sell it to someone else. When rights are issued, they are usually traded (for the short period until they expire) on the same exchange as the stock or other security to which they apply.

Warrants

A *warrant* resembles a right in that it is issued by a company and gives the holder the option of buying the stock (or other security) of the company from the company itself for a specified price. But a warrant has a longer life—often several years, sometimes without limit. As with rights, warrants are negotiable (meaning that they can be sold by the owner to someone else), and some warrants are traded on the major exchanges.

PART III
THE STOCK
MARKET IN
BRIEF

17

A STOCK MARKET PRIMER— WHAT'S WHAT

For those of you who are not as familiar with how the stock market works as you would like to be, here are some explanations that may be useful. (For more information, see the No-Nonsense Financial Guide, *Understanding the Stock Market*.)

What Is a Share of Stock?

A share of stock is a piece of paper representing a share of ownership in a corporation. The more shares you own in any given corporation, the bigger your percentage of ownership. Obviously, in a corporation like A.T.&T. or I.B.M., your percentage will be extremely small.

Many small family-owned businesses, as well as some larger companies, are *privately held*, which means that their stock or ownership is not available for purchase by the public. But it's estimated that perhaps 50,000 corporations have some stock out in public hands, including about 1,500 listed for trading on the New York Stock Exchange.

Rights of Stockholders

A corporation is a separate legal entity that is responsible for its own debts and obligations. The individual owners of the corporation—called *stockholders* or *shareholders*—are not liable for the corporation's obligations. This concept is known as *limited liability*, because the potential liability of the shareholder for corporate debts is limited to the amount he or she paid for the shares. This legal protection has made possible the growth of giant corporations, and has allowed millions of stockholders to feel secure in their position as corporate owners. All that they have at risk is what they paid for their shares—they can't be hauled into court to put up more money if the corporation fails.

As a stockholder (owner) of a corporation, you have certain basic rights in proportion to the number of shares you own. You have the right to vote for the election of directors, who control the company and appoint management. If the company makes profits and the directors decide to pay part of these profits to shareholders as *dividends*, you have a right to receive your proportionate share. And if the corporation is sold or liquidates, you have a right to your proportionate share of the proceeds.

New York Stock Exchange

Stocks are bought and sold on many different stock exchanges, but the largest and most important exchange, and the one usually referred to when one talks about the "stock market," is the New York Stock Exchange (NYSE). The NYSE is the major trading place for the shares of America's largest corporations, from Exxon to I.B.M. to General Motors to Sears, and over 1,500 corporations trade their stock on the NYSE. The NYSE also trades bonds and certain other securities, but stocks are the main show.

Other Exchanges

While the NYSE is the prime marketplace where stocks of most leading U.S. corporations are traded, there are other marketplaces for common stocks as well.

The American Stock Exchange ("AMEX"), also located in New York City, is the prime market for several hundred stocks, mostly of companies smaller than those represented on the NYSE.

There are also regional exchanges, of which the best known are the Pacific, Midwest, Boston and Philadelphia exchanges. A sizeable portion of their trading volume is in "NYSE stocks" that are dually listed on the regional exchanges. In addition, each of these exchanges has its own listings, often of companies in that particular geographical area.

Volume of Trading

In total volume of common stock trading, the other exchanges are small compared with the NYSE. Trading on the NYSE in 1986 averaged about 140 million shares per trading day, or *over $5 billion* daily. By comparison, daily trading on the AMEX was roughly 12 million shares a day (about $175 million), and all the other exchanges combined accounted for over 20 million shares daily (about $750 million).

The above figures do not reflect the total importance of certain exchanges. For example, the AMEX and certain of the regional exchanges have become major factors in the trading of stock *options*, and for many of the brokers on those exchanges, this trading has become more profitable than executing stock transactions. But common stock trading is, in a very real sense, the principal attraction, and the NYSE continues to predominate.

The Over-the-Counter Market

There is one marketplace in which the volume of common stock trading begins to approach that of the NYSE. In 1986, trading of common stocks *over-the-counter* or *OTC*—that is, *not* on any organized exchange—exceeded 110 million shares daily. Since many of the stocks are low-priced, the *dollar* volume was further behind that on the NYSE, but the figure is still impressive.

What is the over-the-counter market? Actually, the term covers all securities trading that is *not* done on a registered exchange. Most securities other than common stocks are traded over-the-counter. For example, the vast market in U.S. government securities is an over-the-counter market. So is the money market—the market in which all sorts of short-term debt obligations are traded daily in tremendous quantities. Likewise the municipal or tax-exempt market—the market for long- and short-term borrowings by state and local governments. And most large transactions in corporate bonds also take place over-the-counter, despite the fact that many of these bonds are listed on the NYSE (where small individual transactions often are executed).

As there is no physical trading floor, over-the-counter trading is accomplished through vast telephone and other electronic networks that link traders as closely as if they were seated in the same room. With the help of computers, price quotations from dealers in Seattle, San Diego, Atlanta and Philadelphia can be flashed on a single screen. Dedicated telephone lines link the more active traders. Confirmations are delivered electronically rather than through the mail.

Dealers thousands of miles apart who are complete strangers execute trades in the thousands or even millions of dollars based on thirty seconds of phone conversation and the knowledge that each is a securities dealer registered with the National Association of Securities Dealers (NASD), the industry self-regulatory organization that also supervises OTC trading. No matter how much the price fluctuates or how much one party later regrets the deal, each knows that any trade made will be honored. When you place an order with your broker for an OTC stock, this remarkable network goes to work for you.

18

A STOCK MARKET PRIMER—
WHO'S WHO

You already are familiar with full-service and discount stockbrokers; this chapter will introduce you to some of the other players in the securities business.

Investment Advisers

Investment advisers give investment advice in exchange for a fee which is usually based on the size of the account being advised or managed. Bank trust departments do a very large business functioning, in effect, as investment advisers. There are also many independent advisory firms—you may have heard the names of some of the large ones, such as Loomis-Sayles, T. Rowe Price, and Scudder, Stevens & Clark.

Most of these advisers don't find it economical to serve the average person. The minimum account size they accept may be $100,000, or $500,000, or even higher. Still, it will be a help to you to understand how they function.

The adviser can work for you on a "non-discretionary" or a "discretionary" basis. In a *non-discretionary* arrangement, the adviser consults with the client and advises about each decision, but the client actually makes the decision. It is probably now more common for the adviser to have *discretion*, that is, to be given the authority to act on behalf of the client. This arrangement makes more sense if the adviser is doing a professional job and if the client is inexperienced. To put it in plain terms, if you are using an adviser, the best course probably is to follow his or her advice, watch the results, and fire the adviser if the results aren't good.

Note that if you are using an adviser who is only an adviser, you still need a broker actually to execute transactions. The advisory firm will usually be glad to take care of the brokerage arrangements if you so desire. But be careful. Many advisory firms have established relationships with full-service brokerage firms. All you should need for your trades is straight brokerage service, and a discount broker should be perfectly adequate unless you are trading in such large quantities, or in such inactive stocks, that you need the extra effort and discretion offered by a full-service broker.

Floor Broker

Once you place an order with your registered representative (RR), your order is relayed by telephone or computer to the *floor broker*. It is the floor broker who actually executes your order in a high-pressured and exhaustingly tense job. The trading floor of the NYSE is huge and is dotted with numerous locations called *trading posts*. The floor broker goes to the trading post where the specific stock you are interested in trading is bought and sold and finds out which other brokers have orders from clients to buy or sell that stock, and at what prices. Your order may be executed within seconds after it is placed.

The Specialist

The Exchange tries to preserve price continuity—which means that if a stock has been trading at, say, 35, the next buyer or seller should be able to execute an order within a fraction of that price (unless some major news has intervened to change the market situation for that stock or for the whole market). But what if a buyer comes in when no other broker wants to sell close to the last price? Or vice versa for a seller? How is price continuity preserved? Enter another individual, the *specialist*.

The specialist is an exchange member charged with a special function, that of maintaining continuity in the price of specific stocks. The specialist does this by standing ready to buy shares at a price reasonably close to the last recorded sale price when someone wants to sell and there is a lack of buyers, and to sell when there is a lack of sellers and someone wants to buy. For each listed stock, there are one or more specialist firms assigned to perform this stabilizing function. Some of the specialist firms are large and are assigned to many different stocks. The Exchange and the SEC are particularly interested in the specialist function, and trading by the specialists is closely monitored to make sure that they are helping to stabilize the markets and not simply making profits for themselves. Since a specialist may at any time be called on to buy and hold substantial amounts of stock, the specialist firms must be well capitalized.

Block Traders

In today's markets, where multi-million-dollar trades by institutions (i.e., banks, money market funds, mutual funds, etc.) have become common, the specialist can no longer absorb all of the large blocks of stock offered for sale, nor supply the large blocks being sought by institutional buyers.

But the securities industry has a history of coming up with creative solutions to trading problems. Over the last several years, there has been a rapid growth in *block trading* by large brokerage firms and other firms in the securities industry. If an institution wants to sell a large block of stock, these firms will conduct an expert and rapid search for possible buyers; if not enough buying interest is found, the block trading firm will fill the gap by buying shares itself, taking the risk of owning the shares and being able to dispose of them subsequently at a profit. If the institution wants to buy rather than sell, the process is reversed.

In a sense, these firms are fulfilling the same function as the specialist, but on a much larger scale. They are stepping in to buy and own stock temporarily when offerings exceed demand and vice versa.

So the specialists and the block traders perform similar stabilizing functions, though the block traders have no official role and have no motive other than to make a profit. A specialist or block trader can go through anxious days after buying a large quantity of a stock if the price goes down. Sometimes a block may be sold at a substantial loss.

Knowing when to buy or sell a block, and what price to pay—and making up one's mind in a matter of minutes or even seconds—makes this a high-paid, tension-packed job. And while it's correctly said that the institutions now dominate trading, the extent to which any single institutional order will affect trading and jar prices is, mercifully, kept down by creative arrangements that absorb shocks to the market and emphasize continuity.

The NYSE and the Computer Age

While the Exchange thrives on human functions, it is dependent on today's electronic magic. Electronic screens in every brokerage office, which have made the old "ticker tape" obsolete, report the day's transactions in an unending stream. The push of a button will call up the record of the day's trading in any stock, and the latest prices being bid and asked for the stock. The stock market averages are calculated in a matter of seconds continuously throughout the day and are flashed around the world over these same systems.

The Exchange has also modernized in smaller ways. Years ago, when you bought shares of a stock, you or your broker took possession of one or more *stock certificates*—elegant pieces of paper which proved your ownership of the shares. They were a nuisance to store safely, and had to be surrendered when it was time to *sell* the shares. Every Wall Street back office had its staff of "runners" or messengers who were kept busy delivering stock certificates to be bought or sold. The certificates still move occasionally, but most changes in ownership are now accomplished by computer entries, and the runners now have less to do.

GLOSSARY

Adviser See Investment Adviser.

AMEX The American Stock Exchange.

Asked Price (or Asking Price) The price at which a dealer offers to sell a security.

Asset Any property owned.

Asset Management Account A versatile brokerage account usually including margin credit and providing for dividends, interest, and the proceeds of any sales to be swept into a money market account where they earn a good interest rate. Cash in the account often can be accessed by credit cards and/or checks.

At the Market An order to buy or sell at the best price the broker can get for you at the time your order is placed.

Balance Sheet The financial statement showing a company's assets, liabilities, and net worth (the net equity of its owners).

Bear An investor who expects the stock market (or a particular stock) to go down.

Bid Price The price at which a dealer offers to buy a security.

Big Board The New York Stock Exchange.

Block Trading Trading in large "blocks" of securities, usually by institutional investors.

Blue Chips A phrase used to describe stocks of leading companies of the highest quality.

Bond A long-term debt security issued by a government or corporation promising repayment of a given amount by a given date, plus interest.

Broker-Dealer See Brokerage Firm.

Brokerage Firm A term including several types of firms in the securities business who usually do business with the public.

Brokers' Call Loan Rate The rate at which stockbrokers borrow money from the banks, using the securities they hold as collateral. Usually below the banks' prime loan rate.

Bull An investor who expects the stock market (or a particular stock) to go up.

Call An option to buy.

Capital Gain The profit from sale of a security or other asset at a price above its cost.

Cash Account A brokerage account in which you pay in full for what you buy—in contrast to a margin account, where you can borrow part of the cost of the securities.

Churning Unnecessarily frequent trading by a broker for the purpose of generating higher commissions.

Common Stock A security representing a share of ownership in a corporation.

Common Stock Fund A mutual fund investing primarily in common stocks.

Confirm The written confirmation of a trade, sent after execution.

Convertible Bond A bond that can be converted into another security, usually common stock.

Corporate Bond A bond issued by a corporation. See Bond.

Corporation A legal entity whose owners, called stockholders or shareholders, enjoy limited liability.

Dealer See Broker-Dealer.

Debenture A type of corporate bond.

Diversification The practice of spreading investments over several different securities to reduce risk.

Dividend A share of earnings paid to a stockholder by a corporation.

Dollar Cost Averaging Investing equal amounts of money at regular intervals.

Equity Ownership interest in an asset.

Financial Futures Contracts to buy or sell various types of instruments at a future date.

Floor Broker A broker who actually executes trading orders on the floor of an exchange.

Good Till Canceled (GTC) A limit order which stays on the books until it is executed or until you cancel it.

Good the Day (Week or Month) A limit order which is valid for that day only, or for a week or a month.

Investment Adviser An individual or organization in the business of giving investment advice. Investment advisers must be registered with the SEC.

Investment Company A company in which many investors pool their money for investment. Mutual funds are the most popular type.

Individual Retirement Account (IRA) A tax-advantaged retirement plan for individuals with earned income.

Joint Tenants with Right of Survivorship A type of ownership of an asset where each party owns the entire asset during their lives and the survivor ends up owning the asset solely.

Keogh Plan A tax-advantaged retirement plan for self-employed individuals.

Limit Order A trading order that authorizes a purchase only if the price dips to a specified level, or a sale only if the price rises to a specified level.

Load The sales charge or commission charged on purchase of some mutual funds.

Long In the securities industry, you are "long" a security when you own it.

Maintenance Level The required amount of cash and/or securities in a margin account.

Margin, Margin Account A type of brokerage account in which you can borrow against the value of the securities you own, either to buy additional securities or to provide cash.

Margin Call The demand by a broker for additional cash or securities to fund a margin account when your equity in the account declines near the minimum allowed by the firm.

Market Not Held Order The phrase means that the broker is not held to take the first available offer or bid, but has discretion to wait and possibly to negotiate if he or she thinks that a better price may be obtainable.

Market Order An order to buy or sell immediately at the best price available.

Money Market Fund A mutual fund that aims at maximum safety, liquidity, and a constant price for its shares.

Municipal Bond A bond issued by a state or local government. The interest is exempt from federal income tax.

Mutual Fund An open-end investment company that pools the investments of many investors to provide them with professional management, diversification and other advantages.

NASD The National Association of Securities Dealers, Inc. A broad industry organization that, among other things, regulates over-the-counter trading.

NASDAQ The NASD automated quotation system, which tabulates and reports on trading of leading over-the-counter stocks.

No-load Fund A mutual fund that sells its shares at net asset value, without any commission.

NYSE The New York Stock Exchange.

Odd Lot A lot of less than 100 shares of stock.

Open-end Investment Company A mutual fund. Technically called open-end because the fund stands ready to sell new shares to investors or to buy back shares submitted for redemption.

Open Order   An order to buy or sell a security that remains in effect until executed or specifically canceled.

Option   A right to buy or sell a specific security at a predetermined price for a given period of time.

Over-the-Counter (OTC)   An over-the-counter stock is a stock not listed on any exchange. Over-the-counter trading is all trading done other than on the exchanges.

Par Value   An arbitrary accounting value given to a stock; of no practical importance.

Portfolio   The total list of investment securities owned by an individual or institution.

Preferred Stock   A type of stock that is entitled to dividends at a specified rate to be paid before any dividends can be paid on the company's common stock.

Price-Earnings Ratio (or Price-Earnings Multiple)   The ratio of the price per share of a stock to its annual earnings per share.

Principal   The capital or main body of an investment, as distinguished from the income earned on it.

Prospectus   The official document describing a security being offered to the public and offering the security for sale. (Every mutual fund must have an annually updated prospectus.)

Put   An option to sell.

Quotation, Quote   A report of the current bid and asked prices on a security.

Registered Representative   A brokerage firm representative who has passed the necessary exam and qualifications to recommend securities and to take orders from the public.

Rights   Usually, a short-term option that a corporation gives its shareholders to purchase new securities, usually at a favorable price.

Round Lot   The normal trading unit of 100 shares of a stock; or a multiple of 100.

R.R.   A registered representative.

Seat   A membership on an exchange.

SEC   The U.S. Securities and Exchange Commission: the federal agency charged with regulating the securities markets and the investment industry.

Securities Investor Protection Corporation (SIPC)   A nonprofit organization that protects securities investors from possible financial failure of a member stockbroker.

Security General term meaning stocks, bonds and other investment instruments.

Settlement Date The date on which payment is due for a security trade; for stocks, ordinarily five business days after the trade date.

Short Sale, Selling Short A trading technique in which you borrow a security and sell it, in the hope that the price of the security will go down so that you can then buy the security back more cheaply and deliver it to repay the loan, making a profit.

Specialist A special type of broker—assigned to make a market in a particular stock or stocks.

Stock A security representing an ownership interest in a corporation.

Stock Certificate A piece of paper evidencing ownership of a particular number of shares of stock.

Stop Limit Order A trading instruction where your order becomes a limit order rather than a market order once the market price goes through the "stop" price.

Stop Order A type of trading order usually used to protect a profit or limit a loss. A stop order in a particular stock becomes a market order when the market price of the stock reaches or sells through a specified "stop" price.

Street Name Securities held in "street name" are registered in the name of the brokerage firm, rather than in name of the customer.

Tape The electronic screen or other device on which stock exchange transactions are shown in sequence as they occur.

Tenants in Common A form of joint ownership without a right of survivorship.

Ticker See Tape.

Trade (Verb) To buy or sell a security. (Noun) The purchase or sale of a security.

Trade Date The date on which a securities trade is executed.

Warrant An option to purchase a security (usually from the issuing company) for a specified price and for a specified period of time.

Yield The return on an investment. In securities, the dividends or interest received, usually expressed as an annual percentage of either the current market value or the cost of the investment.

ABOUT THE AUTHORS

PHYLLIS C. KAUFMAN, the originator of the *No-Nonsense Guides*, is a Philadelphia attorney and theatrical producer. A graduate of Brandeis University, she was an editor of the law review at Temple University School of Law. She is listed in *Who's Who in American Law*, *Who's Who of American Women*, and *Foremost Women of the Twentieth Century*.

ARNOLD CORRIGAN, noted financial expert, is the author of *How Your IRA Can Make You a Millionaire* and is a frequent guest on financial talk shows. A senior officer of a large New York investment advisory firm, he holds Bachelor's and Master's degrees in economics from Harvard and has written for *Barron's* and other financial publications.